MOTOR MAYHEM

ENDURANCE RACING

KENNY ABDO

Fly!
An Imprint of Abdo Zoom
abdobooks.com

abdobooks.com

Published by Abdo Zoom, a division of ABDO, P.O. Box 398166, Minneapolis, Minnesota 55439.

Printed in the United States of America, North Mankato, Minnesota.
052023
092023

THIS BOOK CONTAINS RECYCLED MATERIALS

Photo Credits: Alamy, Getty Images, Shutterstock
Production Contributors: Kenny Abdo, Jennie Forsberg, Grace Hansen
Design Contributors: Candice Keimig, Neil Klinepier

Library of Congress Control Number: 2022946921

Publisher's Cataloging-in-Publication Data

Names: Abdo, Kenny, author.
Title: Endurance racing / by Kenny Abdo
Description: Minneapolis, Minnesota : Abdo Zoom, 2024 | Series: Motor mayhem | Includes online resources and index.
Identifiers: ISBN 9781098281434 (lib. bdg.) | ISBN 9781098282134 (ebook) | ISBN 9781098282486 (Read-to-me ebook)
Subjects: LCSH: Automobiles, Racing--Juvenile literature. | Vehicles--Juvenile literature. | Endurance sports--Juvenile literature.
Classification: DDC 796.72--dc23

TABLE OF CONTENTS

ENDURANCE RACING

With long distances and high stakes, endurance racing has had fans on the edge of their seats for over 100 years!

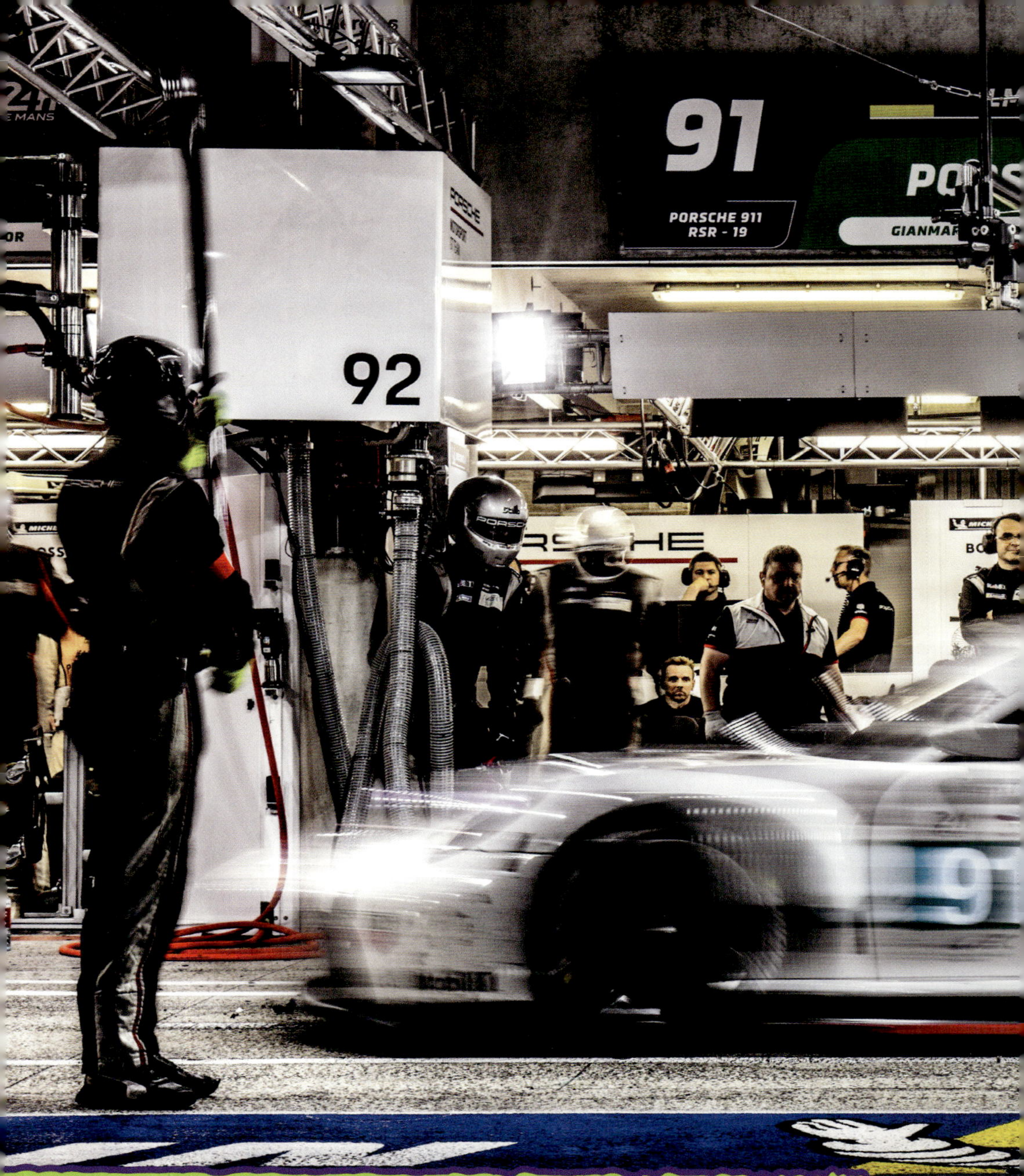

Each car used is built to be fast and durable. The thing that sets a car apart is its driver.

The **motorsport** tests not just the driver's **stamina**, but their skills on the track.

START YOUR ENGINES

Ever since the car's invention, people have found ways to race it! Early competitions saw rough roads and speeds of just 12 miles per hour (20 kph).

The first endurance race was held in 1900. Known as the Coppa Florio, drivers raced along the Italian coast for 115 miles (185 km). From then on, the race for the best was on!

MAYHEM

Endurance races can include teams of two to four drivers. Drivers attempt to go a set distance the fastest. Sometimes the race is to go the farthest in a set time.

FORD
FORD
Ferrari
PRO
SINGHA
HUBLOT
UPS
MICHELIN
SMP RACING
TOYOTA
HY

Huge names such as Ferrari, Lamborghini, and Porsche, build endurance cars. The cars improve each year to be better, faster, and tougher!

During the race, drivers must make **pit stops** to **service** and refuel their car. Drivers also swap out. Each driver takes about a 1-hour **stint** before swapping out.

RuRoc
OMP
90

The toughest endurance races are the **12 Hours of Sebring**, **24 Hours of Le Mans**, and **24 Hours of Daytona**. Teams who accomplish winning all three earn the Triple Crown title!

24h
LE MANS
11-12 JUIN 2022
AUTOMOBILE CLUB DE L'OUEST

BURNOUT

While endurance racing has been around for decades, it continues to take its drivers and the fans on one wild ride!

GLOSSARY

12 Hours of Sebring – a yearly motorsport endurance race held at Sebring International Raceway in Florida.

24 Hours of Daytona – a sports car endurance race held annually at Daytona International Speedway in Daytona Beach, Florida.

24 Hours of Le Mans – a car race held annually near the town of Le Mans, France. It is the world's oldest endurance racing event.

motorsport – a sport involving the racing of motor vehicles, like cars and motorcycles.

pit stop – when a car stops in for servicing and refueling during a race.

service – maintenance of a car to make sure it can run at its best.

stamina – the ability to take on a physical or mental effort for a long time.

stint – a portion of the race between pit stops.

ONLINE RESOURCES

Booklinks
NONFICTION NETWORK
FREE! ONLINE NONFICTION RESOURCES

To learn more about endurance racing, please visit **abdobooklinks.com** or scan this QR code. These links are routinely monitored and updated to provide the most current information available.

INDEX